Peter Riley

WYTHENSHAWE HALL

– And The Tatton Family –

P & D Riley

First published in 1987
This revised edition first published 1999

P & D Riley
12 Bridgeway East,
Cheshire,
WA7 6LD
England

© 1987 and 1999 by Peter Riley

ISBN: 1 874712 38 7

British Library Cataloguing in Publication Data
A catalogue Record for this book is available from the British Library

All rights reserved. No part of this publication may be reproduced, stored in a retrieval system, or transmitted, in any form or by any means, electronic, mechanical, photocopying, recording or otherwise, without the permission of the publisher and the copyright owner.

Printed in England by
Walter Brown Printers, 92 Newton Road, Lowton, Warrington WA3 1DG

Introduction

Wythenshawe Hall, situated about six miles south of Manchester city centre is well worth a visit. Not only is this a place of considerable historical interest and importance, but a place of beauty too. To walk around the ancient hall is to travel back in time, and to walk around the lovely gardens at the rear of the hall is to capture solitude in a delightful setting.

Of course it is best to visit the hall and gardens on a weekday if you want to capture the atmosphere at its best, for summer weekends do tend to attract considerable crowds to the park. May and early June in particular are excellent for appreciating the gardens at the rear of the hall, for they are then a marvellous splash of colour. Many varieties of well established Rhododendron are then in full bloom, and these undoubtedly are worth seeing.

But Wythenshawe Hall itself, which has undergone recent renovations due to that scourge of old buildings dry rot, is still a fascinating building. It is possible to get an idea of how the Tatton family, who owned the hall for 600 years, lived.

If atmosphere is all important for re-living past events, then let me assure you that an overcast, wet day is ideal! With no sunshine outside to distract you, it is possible to really concentrate on the past, and you'll probably be glad that you're inside on such a foul day.

Not intended to be a room by room guide to Wythenshawe Hall but a history of the family itself, it is hoped that this book will serve to offer a useful insight into the long and distinguished service offered to this part of the North of England by the Tatton family

Peter Riley

Acknowledgements

No book, however modest, can be published without the assistance of several people, and this is particularly true of local history publications. Therefore I thank the following for their help.

Susan Hall whose meticulous research when co-authoring another book titled *The Story of Wythenshawe* many years ago enabled me to build up sufficient files to produce the story of the Tatton family of Wythenshawe Hall.

The late Mrs Maud Tatton who not only supplied lots of useful background material during the research but also loaned photographs for copying.

Mrs Catherine Broun, eldest daughter of Robert Henry Grenville and Maud Tatton who offered so much help when asked and who also loaned priceless family photographs which we have used in this book and which have been published here for the first time.

The Local Studies Unit at Manchester Central Library.

Mrs Margaret McAndrew of Dollar Sub-Post Office in Scotland.

Thanks also to Adam Riley, Donna Riley, Elaine Jolly and Peter Reeves for their help, and in the revision of this book thanks are due to Anthea Jarvis of Manchester Art Gallery for her help in correcting historical errors which had crept into the original edition.

One

WYTHENSHAWE Hall. A lovely tudor building six miles south of Manchester city centre was the home of the Tatton family for 600 years.

Successive generations lived and died at the hall; action in the English Civil War was seen there; tenant farmers visited the estate to pay their respects as well as their rent to the Lord of the Manor.

First mention of the Tatton family is shown in records dating from 1290, which show that they were then living in the hamlet of Kenworthy, approximately one mile from the site of the present hall. The Mascy family were then lords of the manor and almost certainly lived in a house on or close to the site of the present hall. The Tatton's, despite their lack of prominence at that time, nevertheless held some influence and this is proved by a Charter witnessed in 1316 by William de Tatton and his sons Robert and Richard. Without influence there is little possibility of them being called upon to include their signatures to such an important document which was the transfer of certain parcels of land from Lord of the Manor, Thomas de Mascy, to his son William and to William de Baggelegh.

Only 32 years later a Charter dated August 1348 was also witnessed by Tatton members, and in 1370 a Charter drawn up by Alice de Mascy, only daughter of William, clearly shows that lands were being handed over to Robert de Tatton of Kenworthy, possibly as part of a marriage settlement.

Thus, without fear of contradiction, records clearly show that the Tatton family line and influence within Wythenshawe started from 1370 and lasted for the next 556 years until the Tatton family left the hall and estate for the last time in 1926.

By 1396 Alice de Mascy (Tatton?) was dead, but in the quarter century they were together, three sons were produced with the respective names of Robert (who died young), Thomas and John. The names Robert and Thomas were to become a standard form of moniker within the Tatton family, although William was another favourite.

One of the bedrooms at Wythenshawe Hall pictured in 1926. the year the Tatton family left

At the time of the 'take over' by the Tatton's most of England was covered with forests and pasture lands, and Wythenshawe must have been very remote. To those living within what is now Wythenshawe Hall the solitude would only have been broken by the large staff, although farming sounds would have also broken the silence since the family were keen growers of their own produce. And the village of Northenden (much older than Wythenshawe) was only a mile away.

For several decades no records are available to show what was happening in Wythenshawe, and it is only through the Tatton family tree that we can see events.

By 1418 the Wythenshawe estate was in the hands of William de Tatton who subsequently passed on the property to his son Nicholas Tatton. He was undoubtedly a man of considerable energy, for he later became Baron of the Exchequer of Chester, a high office at that period. Indeed this office was held by the Tatton family for several generations and we can safely assume that from this period the Tatton name was becoming well known and respected throughout the whole county of Cheshire.

By the late 15th century two Tatton brothers, William and John, added to the family reputation within the county, for in 1484 William became Baron of the Exchequer in Chester and in 1505 he became Vice-Chamberlain of Chester, thus becoming known as William Tatton of Chester. Brother John followed William in gaining titles. He became Sheriff of Chester in 1503 and Baron of the Exchequer in about 1530. Because of these connections he became known as John Tatton of Chester.

It was shortly after this that the Wythenshawe name became into prominent use. Although William was the eldest brother, and thus heir apparent, it was left to John to carry on the family name. He married Margaret, daughter of Ralph Davenport of Chester (who was three times Mayor of the city) and this union produced three children, one of which was a boy named Robert. He became heir apparent and in later life added considerably to the family estates as well as to the Tatton dynasty itself.

By his marriage to Dorothy, fourth daughter of George Booth of Dunham Massey, Robert Tatton of Wythenshawe as he was then known became the father or eleven children - seven sons and four daughters. With such a large population increase it is little wonder that Wythenshawe Hall became the focal point of the Tatton family, thus strengthening the already strong ties of past centuries.

This Robert Tatton was also the first recorded member of the family to take over 'The Peele' a small manor house in the area then known as Northern Etchells. The house, later better known as 'Peel Hall' was situated two miles from the main hall at Wythenshawe, was to be used as a dower house, a function it never achieved during Robert's lifetime. 'The Peele' was demolished in the early 19th century and a farmhouse built on the site which was itself demolished in 1975.

After his death in 1579 Robert was buried in Northenden Churchyard, a request he made in his will, and it is interesting to note that the Tatton family had their own chapel in the ancient church.

On the subject of Robert's will it is interesting to pause for a moment and look at some of the contents of that document. More than anything else, it is probably true to say that a will provides an ideal insight into the workings of a large family such as the Tattons, and the will of Robert Tatton of Wythenshawe Hall is a good example of this. The will, for example, shows that Robert owned not only Wythenshawe Hall and surrounding land, but also the Manor of Etchells (The Peele) and lands near Chester, Altrincham and Flintshire in North Wales.

He bequeathed his property (with the exception of Wythenshawe Hall and surrounding parklands) to his son and heir, William, and stated that his wife, Dorothy, should retain possession of Wythenshawe Hall since 'The Peele' was not sufficiently built at that period to be used as a dower house. In addition, says the will, the manor house at Peel Hall was too far away for Robert's wife to be able to travel to Northenden for regular church services, or as the language of the time says..."she beinge not able to travel so farr in her olde yeres to here God's devyne service."

Robert also stated that his widow was to have as much land as she required to keep 12 cattle for her lifetime, though there was a stipulation that she would have to pay her son William rent for this land since he was now legal heir to the family fortunes. Dorothy was also given 'The Peele' and surrounding lands (now Peel Hall estate) for life, with the same arrangement of rent being payable to William. The total value of Robert's possessions on his death were stated as £754. 8s. 6d, a large amount for 1579.

In 1606 another Robert Tatton was born, and during his lifetime there were to be astonishing changes at Wythenshawe Hall.

Randle Holme's sketch of the memorial in Northenden Church in 1579 to Robert Tatton, his wife Dorothy and their eleven children. The clothing in the sketch is of typical Elizabethan design. The family crests of both the Tatton and Booth families are also shown

Two

When Robert Tatton was only ten years old his father, William, unfortunately drowned in the River Mersey, and since Robert was the only male child he became heir to the Wythenshawe estate, but being a minor he was made a ward of the king, Charles I, a small event in itself but one which was to have serious political impact on his later years. On January 9, 1628, aged 22, he married at Bowdon Anne Brereton, third daughter of William Brereton of Ashley, and the couple settled down at Wythenshawe Hall, Robert having by that time inherited his estate on his Coming of Age.

On October 23, 1642, the English Civil War broke out and Robert joined the Royalist side in what was to be a hard and long struggle against the Parliamentarian forces of Oliver Cromwell. And only months after Charles I had raised his royal standards at Nottingham, thus starting the war, Wythenshawe Hall came under siege as Cromwell's local commander, Colonel Robert Duckenfield, ordered his men to take the hall and its wealth.

Taking Wythenshawe Hall, however, was not as easy as it first looked, for having received advance information that the 'Roundheads' were advancing Robert Tatton quickly called about him all his domestic staff, farm workers and many of his royalist friends from nearby Didsbury, Northenden, Baguley, Sharston, Altrincham, Hale and other parts of Northern Etchells. In all a total of more than 50 men were used in the defence of the hall. between November 21, 1643 and February 27, 1644.

There have been many accounts published on the siege of Wythenshawe Hall, but the following, written at the time, is perhaps the most interesting. It begins at a point where Parliamentarian troops, having been through Northenden hamlet ransacking and destroying the windows and furniture at St Wilfred's Church turned their attention to Wythenshawe Hall.

"*The Master Tatton's turn came next. We heard, day by day, of the attempts that were made to reduce the hall, but all attempts were in vain.*

"*It stood out bravely against the rebels, although at one time they nearly gained possession, and in attempting an entrance they killed six of the soldiers defending the great hall, who were buried in a decent manner in the* garden at the back of the house, the rebels refusing a truce even for a day, that the bodies might be taken, as was fit, and laid in consecrated ground with the service of the church read over them.

"There was in the house a Withenshaw girl whose name was Mary Webb. She had been brought up by the family, but had nothing in peculiar in her disposition, save that, perhaps she was more noted for her gentleness of manner and smoothness of temper than for anything else.

"It happened that one of the six men who were killed in the attack by Captain Adams (second in command to Duckenfield) was affianced to poor Mary Webb, and his death aroused strange feelings in her mind, so that she resolved to have her vengeance of the man that had caused the loss of her lover. I commend not an act of revenge, but I speak as it happened.

"On a Sunday in February this Captain Adams was sitting on a wall near the house, little thinking of danger near him, when the girl Webb, having borrowed a musket from some of the parties within the house, approached to a proper distance, and then, levelling the musket at the captain, shot him dead.

Colonel Robert Duckenfield. Commander of the Parliamentarian forces which beseiged Wythenshawe Hall in the Civil War

"It was much talked of at the time, and the girl was applauded by some and blamed by others, according to the view they took of the deed.

"The body of the captain was taken the same day to Stockport, where it was buried. After this event two cannons were brought from Manchester, and the house reduced. When taken the ammunition was gone, and but little provisions left.

"My good patron, Mr. Tatton, is living in retirement, at this time, in a distant part of the country, from whence he hopes to come when God has ridded this place of enemies, and I, the writer of these few papers, remain still with my kind friends on the Mersey's banks. All is dark at present, but it will surely have an end." Upon capitulation, an inventory of all goods in possession of Robert Tatton was completed, and the total amount was valued at £1,649. 2s 8d., a considerable amount of money in those days.

When Colonel Duckenfield's men took control of Wythenshawe Hall it was noted that Robert Tatton had escaped. He made his way from Wythenshawe to Chester, where in 1645 he was made High Sheriff of the county of Cheshire. He was still in Chester when that city was besieged by Cromwell's forces and was finally forced into capitulation in February, 1646.

Again Tatton escaped, this time heading for Oxford where he joined the King. He was not in Oxford very long, however, before that city too was attacked. It finally surrendered on June 24, 1646.

Following the defeat of the Royalist armies and the capture of Charles I, Cromwell's forces set about the enormous task of preparing a list of estates which were to be forfeited by those who had been loyal to the Crown.

Robert Tatton's Wythenshawe estate was among those listed. Cromwell, though he was to be ruthless with the king, Charles being executed, was not so ruthless with his followers. In fact many were allowed certain 'privileges', among them the return of forfeited estates on payment of a levy or fine decided by the Cromwellian parliament.

Robert Tatton was so privileged.

When parliament came to Tatton's 'Delinquencie', as it was called, the following summary was drawn up to decide Robert Tatton's fine.

Robert Tatton of Wythenshawe, Esq

"*His Delinquencie, that hee deserted his owne Dwellinge, and went and lived in Oxford whiles it was a Garrison holden for the Kinge againste the Parliament, and was there at the tyme of the surrender, and is to have the benefit of those articles as by Sir Thomas Ffairefax certificate of the 24th of June 1646 doth appeare.*

Hee hath neither taken the Negative Oath nor Convenante, but prayes to be exempt upon the articles of Oxford and the Vote of the House of Commons pursuante..."

This summary goes on for several paragraphs which would do justice the today's lawyers, but the interesting portions are those showing income from the various Tatton holdings within the region. For example, from Wythenshawe and Northenden estates the income was estimated at £140, while rents from Northern Etchells, Kenworthy and Moorside were worth the sum of £58.16s.8d. It was also stated that after the death of his mother, Katherine Nicholls (who was then married to the Reverend William Nicholls, ejected rector of Cheadle, and living at Peel Hall) Robert would inherit lands and property which would bring in £110 a year.

The summary also showed that, according to Tatton, he owed considerable amounts of money, in addition to actual income loss due to the Civil War.

Parliament nevertheless fined Robert Tatton £804.10s.0d, which was reduced to £707.13s.4d by an order dated December 23, 1646.

Robert Tatton was one of the luckier ones in the Civil War. He escaped twice, fought hard against parliament, and lived. He also lived long enough to see peace restored to England, and also to see the restoration of the Monarchy when Charles II took his executed father's place as King.

Tatton was also rewarded by Charles II for his loyalty to the Crown. He was given a pure silver snuff box as a personal gift, and it is fascinating to know that this snuff box is still owned by his descendants.

Robert Tatton died on August 19, 1669, and was buried at Northenden of August 24 of that year.

He had out-lived Oliver Cromwell by eleven years.

Three

In November 1732 the Wythenshawe estate was passed on to one William Tatton (whose father, also called William had just died), and with this inheritance the fortunes of the Tattons of Wythenshawe were to take yet another turn.

William married, in May 1747, Hester, the eldest daughter of John Egerton of Tatton Park near Knutsford, Cheshire. His new bride was also heiress to the estate, and thus the estates of Wythenshawe and Tatton Park were merged.

The marriage of Hester and William lasted 29 years, and ended on April 28, 1776, the day William died. Following her husband's death, Hester resumed the name Egerton and on her death in May, 1780, her only son and heir, also called William, acknowledged Hester's dying wish that the Egerton name be kept alive and this he did by assuming by Royal Licence the name and arms of Egerton.

William (Tatton) Egerton was 31 years of age at the time he took over the Wythenshawe and Knutsford estates; he was also a Member of Parliament, and was married to Frances Maria Fountayne of York. She was the first of four wives! Frances Maria had given birth to three children in four years and she died aged only 26 in 1777.

William's second marriage was to Mary Wilbraham Bootle of Somerset, this marriage produced four children before Mary died in November 1784, aged 24!

Two years after Mary's death, William married for the third time. This time his bride was Anna Maria Armytage of Kirklees, Yorkshire. (Incidentally, Kirklees is famous as the reputed place where legendary outlaw Robin Hood died) This marriage lasted 13 years and Anna Maria died in 1799, having produced only one child who had died in infancy.

Marriage number four was to Charlotte Clara Watkinson of Kent on November 1, 1803. Again misfortune struck this union and Charlotte Clara died only nine months later on August 11, 1804.

William himself died in 1806, and he was succeeded by his eldest surviving son Wilbraham Egerton who became known as Lord Egerton of Tatton. William's second son, Thomas William, took over the Wythenshawe estate, resuming, by Royal Licence, the name Tatton, thus becoming known as Thomas William Tatton of Wythenshawe.

While Wilbraham continued his life as owner of Tatton Park, Thomas was left to continue his life at Wythenshawe Hall.

On October 20, 1807, Thomas married Emma Grey, and by this marriage nine children were born, though only one boy whom he named after himself. Besides his marital and estate duties, Thomas also found time to take on the role of High Sheriff of Cheshire in 1809, thus carrying on an old family tradition.

Thomas William Tatton died on March 2, 1827, leaving the estate to his only son. Thomas was only 43 years old when he died.

The succession of Wythenshawe was taken over by Thomas William's only son, also named Thomas William, and although he was only eleven at the time his early years are shrouded in obscurity. He became in later years, however, a very active man. In 1867 he is shown to be a Churchwarden at St Wilfred's Church in Northenden, and indeed took such an interest in the church that he laid the foundation stone of the present St Wilfred's on April 11, 1874.

When he died on May 10, 1885, an obituary was published in the *Northenden Parish Magazine* which is worth quoting here. It read:

THE DEATH OF MR TATTON OF WYTHENSHAWE

On Sunday Evening, 10th of May, there passed in peace away the spirit of him whom we have for years been privileged to respect as our Squire and to love as our friend. After a short illness - the probable effects of a chill - Mr Thomas William Tatton of Wythenshawe, breathed

Above : Harriet Susan Parker, wife of Thomas William Tatton, and Right: Thomas William Tatton, born 1816, died 1885

his last in the presence of his family. He retained his consciousness to the last and had received with evident satisfaction the sacred ministrations of the Rector, the Rev. Ed.L.Y. Deacle.

Mr Tatton, who was universally beloved to all who knew him, was born 2nd June 1816, his ancestry dating back to the time of Edward II; he was the eldest son of the late Mr Thomas William Tatton...After receiving his education at Eton and at Christ Church, Oxford, Mr Tatton married on 25th January, 1843, Harriet Susan...by whom he had issue, three sons and one daughter. Mr Tatton was a Magistrate and Deputy Lieutenant for the County of Cheshire, having been placed on the Commission of the Peace as early as 1842, and six years later was appointed High Sheriff of the County.

Amongst the earliest of his charitable works were the interest and support he gave to the Blind Asylum at Old Trafford...serving the offices of Chairman of the Committee, Vice President and President. Mr Tatton was senior Feoffee of Chetham's College and Library, and was rarely absent from the meetings of Governors...In going up and down the College yard, he would stop and enter into the interest of the game which the boys happened to be playing at the time. Nothing delighted him more than to have the boys out for a day at Wythenshawe, and let them roam at will through its pleasant park and gardens. He once told, in his charmingly quiet way, a party of 'old boys' whom he had invited to Wythenshawe, how much he and some of his ancestors owed to the memory of Humphrey Chetham for enabling them to hold the estate during the Civil War and the subsequent rule of the Protectorate...Mr Tatton was interred in the family vault, in the Village Church Yard, on Ascension Day, 14th of May, amid the manifestations of heartfelt sorrow. The Church Officers, the Choir, the Ringers, took part in the Funeral Service, which was numerously attended by the Household, Tenantry and Labourers on the Estate.

The above is only an extract from the obituary, but it does say a lot about the singular character of Mr Tatton, who does not fit the role of stern Victorian which we have come to expect from 'Squires' of that period.

With the death of Thomas William Tatton in 1885, the Wythenshawe estate passed into the hands of his eldest son, Thomas Egerton, who was 39 years old at the time.

Thomas Egerton as a young man was quite active, and he too had been educated at Eton and Christ Church, Oxford. In 1877 he had married Essex Mary Cholmondeley, and they had three children: Robert Henry Grenville, born 1883, and two daughters, Alice, born 1877 (died 1929), and Eva Beatrice born 1879.

In 1887-88 Thomas Egerton Tatton is listed as a Churchwarden of Northenden Church, and like so many of his family was very active in this capacity. As he started getting older, however, he became an invalid and he was confined to a bath-chair. He also developed heart problems and had a full time nurse looking after him.

Because of his illness Wythenshawe Hall was to lose the gaiety of earlier years, but not until towards the end of Thomas Egerton's life. Well before that, there were two celebrations in which he took an active interest.

The first, in 1904, was to celebrate the Coming of Age of his only son and heir, Robert Henry Grenville Tatton, better known within family circles as 'Peter'.

Although the birthday was on March 2, 1904, it was in the week beginning September 9, that the first of the celebrations were held. The *Manchester Evening News* published a report on the event, and the following is taken from it:

"This afternoon a garden party was held at Wythenshawe, Northenden, the historical residence of Mr Thomas Egerton Tatton, in celebration of the coming of age of the heir, Mr Robert Henry Grenville Tatton. The guests included Earl Egerton of Tatton and the Duchess of Buckingham, Colonel and Mrs Dixon, Colonel and Mrs Cornwall Legh, Mr. T. F. and Lady Clare Egerton, Lady Leighton, Lord and Lady Newton and the Hon. Miss Legh, the Hon. Alan de Tatton Egerton, MP., and Mrs Egerton, Colonel and Mrs Lonford Brooke, Lady Elphinstone, Mr Coningsby Disraeli, MP., and Mrs Disraeli, Colonel and Mrs Warburton (Arley). All the leading families in the county were represented.

During the week the tenants of Wythenshawe estate have been entertained at the hall, a ball being held and an address and portrait presented to the heir.

Mr R.H.G. Tatton was educated at Eton and subsequently at Christ Church, Oxford. He holds a commission in the Oxfordshire Militia, and is a fine athlete. He is greatly liked by the tenantry and the county people, and congratulations have poured in from all parts..."

The second celebration took place on November 11, 1911. Robert Henry Grenville Tatton married Miss Maud Hamilton, and the following report was published in the *Altrincham Division Advertiser* the day after the wedding.

THE HEIR OF WYTHENSHAWE
Marriage of Mr. R.H.G. Tatton

Considerable interest was taken in Cheshire in the marriage which took place yesterday at St Peter's in the East, Oxford, between Mr Robert Henry Grenville Tatton, only son of Mr and Mrs Tatton, of Wythenshawe, Northenden, Cheshire, and Miss Maud Hamilton, younger daughter of Mrs R.P. Hamilton, Bray, County Wicklow, Ireland. There was a large and fashionable gathering at the ceremony.

The bride, who was given away by her uncle, Willoughby Hamilton, Esq., was charmingly attired in rich ivory satin, veiled in ninon. Some old Brussels lace (the gift of the bridegroom's mother) was draped in fichu style on the bodice, and forming a panel, and on each side were 'boulleonnes' of ninon, and trails of hand made roses and shamrock, graduating in size the full length of the train to the shoulder. She carried a bouquet of white orchids and lilies of the valley, and her ornaments were a string of pearls (the gift of the bridegroom) and a gold bracelet (the gift of the tenants of the Wythenshawe estate).

The bride was attended by five bridesmaids, these being Miss Netty Walker, the Lady Jane Grey, Miss Freya Sykes, Miss Dorothy Hamilton, and Miss Eve Marindin. They wore Romney dresses of soft pale blue satin, the only trimming being a large ostrich feather of the same shade of blue.

The mother of the bride was dressed in white satin charmeuse, veiled with black ninon, fringed with jet, and trimmed with old Brussels applique. She wore a black velvet hat, trimmed with feathers and lace.

The mother of the bridegroom wore a dress of black lace and velvet, over white satin; a black velvet hat, and black velvet stole and muff.

Sir Harry Mainwaring, Bart., of Over Peover Hall, officiated as best man, and Master Sykes and Master Fitzhugh were present as pages, their costumes were black velvet Court suits and capes lined with pale blue.

The service was fully choral, and the officiating clergymen were the Rev. E.M. Walker (fellow of Queen's College) and the Rev. Lowry Hamilton (the rector of Northenden)

A point of much discussion following any wedding is on the subject of presents, and this is particularly true of large and important weddings. The wedding of Robert and Maud Tatton is undoubtedly within this category, and it is hoped the reader will find the following list of presents given to the newly-weds of interest. They are reproduced in this book in full for the first time in any publication thanks to the generosity of the late Mrs Tatton.

BRIDE'S PRESENTS

Bridegroom to bride,	pearl necklace.
Mrs Cunningham,	silver coffee spoons.
Miss Tatton,	gold and pearl bracelet.
Colonel Cholmondeley,	Opal pendant.
Mr and Mrs A.L. Tucker	Indian embroidery.
Miss McMinn,	Irish potato bowl.
Mr and Mrs Edwin Hamilton,	jewelled brooch.
Mr de la Cherois,	brooches and earrings.
Mrs McCormack,	Limerick lace.

Miss Rainey,	cushion.
Mrs Greenwood,	silver candlesticks.
Mrs C.W. Murphy,	blotter and tea cloth.
Master C. Murphy,	pin-cushion.
Miss Beeson,	enamel buckle and buttons.
Miss M.R. Pollock,	pearl bracelet.
Mrs Tatton,	Brussels lace and ostrich feather fan.
The Rev. E.M. and Mrs Walker,	antique crystal pendant.
Mrs and Mrs Bell,	travelling clock.
Mr T. E. Tatton,	fitted suit case.
Mr and Mrs A. E. Knight,	silver ink pot.
Mr R.G Tatton,	emeralds and diamond ring and emerald and diamond pendant.
Miss D. Blizzard,	embroidered cloth.
Miss Hill,	embroidered handkerchief.
The Misses Lenthalls,	silver vases.
Mr and Mrs Bischoff,	cut-glass flower bowl.
Miss Ashe,	Chinese box.
Mrs Dunbar-Buller,	embroidered cloth.
Mr and Mrs White,	antique cups and saucers.
Mrs Manley,	silver asparagus spoon and fork.
The Misses Manly,	pearl and amethyst brooch.
Mrs Lindsay,	embroidered cloth.
Mrs Wills,	large china vase.
Rev. Lowry and Mrs Hamilton,	silver coffee pot.
Miss Bernard,	silver cream jug and sugar bowl.
Messrs Charles and Hugh Hamilton,	silver syphon holder.
Mrs R. P. Hamilton,	silver mustard pot, cheque, travelling rug.
Miss Ormsby,	umbrella.
Mr and Mrs Alfred Hamilton,	breakfast set.
Mr and Mrs A. Kinahan,	silver candlesticks.
Miss B. Worthington,	Irish lace collar.
Mr and Mrs A. Hamilton,	cheque.
The Rev. R. and Mrs Lefroy,	amethyst pendant.
Miss Worthington,	salts bottle.
Mr and Mrs W.J. Hamilton,	cheque and lace handkerchief.
Mrs and the Misses Thompson,	silver muffin dish.
The Rev. and Mrs Roland Scriven,	cheque.
Mrs Warren,	silver calendar.

Mr and Mrs Walker	silver tea knives
Mr and Mrs Olive Kinahan,	cushion.
Mr. R. Tatton,	enamel pendant, watch and chain.
The Hon. Mrs Cholmondeley,	antique paste pair ornaments.
Miss Taylor,	Irish lace handkerchiefs.
Miss H. Hamilton,	book.
Miss L. Hamilton,	Indian cloth.
Miss T. Hamilton,	Bible.
Mr George Mountain,	silver photograph frame.
Lady Jane Grey,	hat pins.
Mrs Blizzard,	silver cream jug.
Mr and Mrs Elvington Balk,	cheque.
The Misses Hamilton,	blotter.
Miss Marriott,	tray.
The Rev. H. B. and Mrs Hamilton,	cheque.
Mrs Firth,	moonstone pendant.
Miss Cholmondeley,	antique inlaid tea caddy.
Mr and Mrs John Haldane,	book.
Mr and Mrs C. H. Thomson,	silver bon-bon dish.
Miss Vernon,	gold wrist watch.
Miss Hamilton,	book.
Mr and Mrs George Hamilton,	gold embroidered scarf.
The Rev. J. C. Hamilton,	book.
Mr and Mrs Ernest Pollock,	pair china vases.
Miss Ffrench,	book.
Mr and Mrs R. H. Bookey,	pair silver candlesticks.
Mr George Pollock,	cheque.
Mrs and the Misses Gahan,	silver tea strainer.
Miss Mary and Miss Helen Blizzard,	tea cosy.
Mr and Mrs Milliken,	handkerchiefs.
Mrs and Miss de la Chelois,	embroidered cloth.
Mr and Mrs Cannan,	cut glass bowl.
Mr and Mrs Hugh Henry,	Amethyst and pearl pendant.
Mrs Hibbert,	case of gold safety pins.
The Pro Provost of Queen's and Mrs Armstrong,	old print.
Mr and Mrs Malcolm Riall,	silver card case.
The Misses Scott,	tea-cloth.
The Misses Marindin,	silver pin-cushion.
Mr J.D. and Miss Netty Walker,	trays.

Major and Mrs Marindin, large silver frames.
Servants at Besselsleigh Rectory and 9 Merton St., tea knives.
Tenants of the Wythenshawe Estates, gold bracelet.

BRIDEGROOM'S PRESENTS

Lack of space does not allow a list of those giving presents to the bridegrooms, but much of the list is repeated within the bride's shown above, however the actual presents he received were as follows:-

Picture and dog, antique mirror, marble clock, claret jug, wine glasses, Sheffield plate salver barometer, cigarette case, pair of china shelves and china figures, carved table, antique gun, silk rug, breakfast dishes, double-handed silver bowl, silver gilt pot-pourri pot, china bowl, cheque, cheque, silver backed hair brushes, weighing machine for writing table, cheque, Elkington plate and tea service, silver hunting card case, set of coloured hunting prints, silver salver, cheque, Norwegian enamel match box, silver biscuit tin, pair of Sheffield plate hand candles, cut-glass inkstand and silver top, chin bowl, carved wooden lid and stand, hunting crop, walking stick, cheque, pair of silver toast racks, seal, pair of Nuremberg decanters, Osterley table tray, cigarette box, cheque, coal box, house linen and cheque, damascus box, cut glass jug, silver inkstand, 'Tantalus spirit decanter, hunting crop, sugar sifter, pair of glass vases, forked back armchair, gold pencil case, cheque, sugar sifter, dessert knives, forks, spoons, pair of Sheffield plate entree dishes, pair of Sheffield plate wine coolers, pepper grinder, silver tea stand and plates, despatch box, 'Tantulus' spirit decanter, reference book and stand, Crown Derby tea set, copper bowl, cigarette box, silver nut basket and two pairs of silver nut crackers, tea set and tray, sugar sifter, fruit bowl, silver sugar basin, seal, pair of double silver candlesticks, Osterley table tray, pair of silver spoons, cheque, silver cigar and cigarette box, Sheffield plate tea caddy, cellarette, silver candlesticks, bridge set, flask, rosewood table, sugar spoon, silver salver and 'The Golly' Thermos flask, clock, table lamp, Bible and book of morning prayers, silver dessert service, electric lamp, old silver cup, arm-chair, silver tea caddy, old print, liqueur glasses, bicycle, brass candlesticks, plate warmers, plate warmers, cheque, umbrella, match boxes.

The list is certainly comprehensive despite the inevitable repeat of certain gifts. However in a house the size of Wythenshawe Hall there would be hardly have been any problem using them all.

Finally within this chapter, it is worth noting some details of the new Mrs Maud Tatton's antecedence, and this is also taken from a document loaned by her some years ago.

Miss Eva Maud Hamilton is the youngest daughter of the late Mr Robert Pollock Hamilton. Her maternal grandfather was the Rev. Alfred Hamilton, D.D., Canon of Christ Church, Dublin, for many years Rector of Taney, who was the grandson of the Right Rev. Hugh Hamilton, Bishop of Ossory, the eldest son of Alexander Hamilton, of Knock, and Newton Hamilton, a member of the Irish Parliament from 1730 to 1757.

A younger brother of the Bishop's was the Baron Hamilton of Hampton Hall, Co. Dublin, whose enlightened efforts for the improvement of the condition of the Irish peasantry are warmly recommended by the famous Arthur young in his 'Tour of Ireland'. This branch of the Hamilton is descended from Sir James Hamilton, of Finnary. Co. Renfrew, son of the first Earl of Anan, who settled in Ireland in the sixteenth century. Mr Robert Pollock Hamilton was a grandson, on his mother's side of the late Lord Chief Baron Pollock.

Four

In 1924 Thomas Egerton Tatton died after a long illness, and the Wythenshawe estate passed into the hands of Robert Henry Grenville Tatton.

He already lived in Wythenshawe Hall with Maud, his wife, and their children, William Grey Maurice, born 1912, Elizabeth Catherine, born 1914, Susan, and Christopher, born 1922. But the winds of change were already blowing across the Wythenshawe landscape, and before long they were to turn into a full-blown storm.

Before Thomas Egerton Tatton had died he had been approached by the City of Manchester who wanted to buy his Wythenshawe lands for housing development. With several centuries of family ties behind him, the old man had strongly resisted. Now the pressure was placed on 'Peter' Tatton's shoulders.

He too resisted the pressures of growing Manchester, but eventually he realised he could not win this battle. In

1926 he finally gave in and sold his estate to Manchester Corporation. They had succeeded where Oliver Cromwell had not!

Tatton sold approximately 2,500 acres to Manchester, but Wythenshawe Hall and 250 acres of parkland were sold instead to Ernest Simon (Later Lord Simon) who generously donated the hall and park to Manchester to be used solely for the public good. By that gesture lovely Wythenshawe Hall and Park were saved from demolition and development respectively.

After Tatton sold Wytheshawe he prepared to leave the family home of 600 years and move with his wife, Maud, and children, to live in Wybunbury, on the Cheshire-Staffordshire border. It was a sad day, not only for the Tatton family but for the tenants of Wythenshawe Hall also. They were unable to comprehend the sudden change to their lives, a change which was to be total.

At Wythenshawe Hall, there remained after the departure of the Tatton's only one man, the old chauffeur named Brownett, who was to serve tea to the new visitors. A far cry indeed from earlier days when the house bustled with life and with staff compromising of a cook, kitchen maid, scullery maid, butler, footman, houseboy, three house-maids, two laundry maids, and personal maids.

The year 1926 was sad in yet another way for Robert and Maud Tatton, for it was also the year in which their son and heir William Grey Maurice Tatton died at Eton. He was 14 years of age, and was buried in the family vault in Northenden. Also in that year, Robert's uncle and hunting companion Reginald Tatton died.

The Tatton family lived in Wybunbury until the close of World War II (During which time they had lost their last son, and heir to the Tatton name, Christopher, who had been killed on the ship H.M.S. Prince of Wales, when it was sunk by the Japanese in December 1941) when they moved to Kent. It was here on March 1, 1962, that Robert Henry Grenville Tatton died, the day before his 79th birthday.

Like so many of his ancestors before him, Mr Tatton's ashes were interred in the family grave in Northenden.

With his death links with 600 years of Tatton history in Wythenshawe were severed for ever.

A Photo Album

Pictured in happy family setting in Wythenshawe Hall in 1912 are Thomas Egerton Tatton (far right), his wife Essex Tatton, Robert Henry Grenville Tatton and his wife Maud and their first born child William Grey Maurice Tatton.

Wytheshawe Hall pictured in 1916, just a decade before the hall was sold

Left: Emma Tatton, daughter of the Hon. John Grey of Groby, 3rd son of Harry, 4th Earl of Stamford. Married 1807 to Thomas William Tatton and died April 28, 1851

Thomas William Tatton, born October 29, 1783, second son of Thomas Tatton Egerton. Reassumed the surname of Tatton by Royal Licence on January 9, 1806, on succeeding to the Wythenshawe Estates.
Died on March 2, 1827. This miniature was painted when he was about 20 years old by his grandmother Hester Egerton of Tatton

Left: William Grey Maurice Tatton, born November 12, 1912, who died at Eton on February 28, 1926. He was the eldest son of R.H.G. and Maud Tatton.

Christopher Tatton, born November 25, 1922, who died in the sinking of the Royal Navy ship H.M Prince of Wales by the Japanese December 10, 1941. He was the last male heir to the Tatton name in Wythenshawe.

Robert Henry Grenville Tatton, better known as Peter, was the last member of the Tatton family to own Wythenshawe Hall and its large estate. He is pictured in 1904 in the uniform of the Oxford and Buckinghamshire Light Infantry, of which he was a Captain

Below: R.H.G. Tatton, 1883 - 1962 last owner of Wythenshawe, pictured at his Coming of Age in 1904

Top: Robert Henry Grenville Tatton pictured in 1931 when he stood to the County Council elections in Wybunbury, Northwich

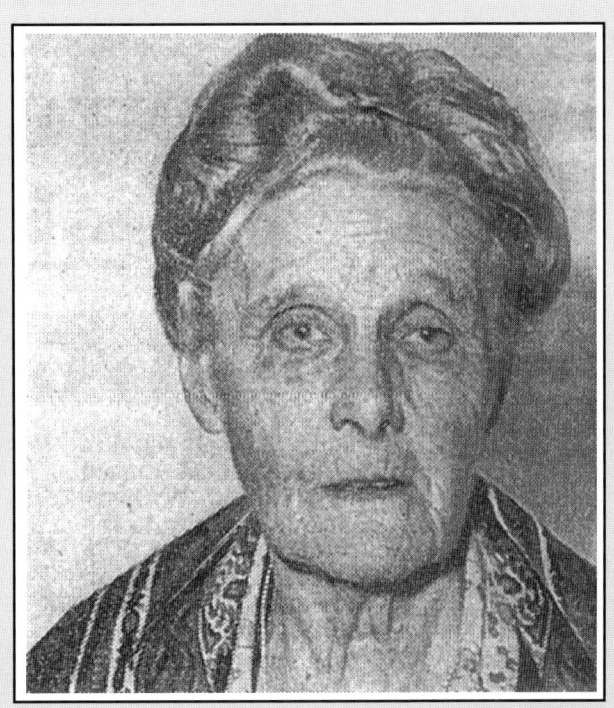

Mrs Maud Tatton, wife of Robert Henry Grenville Tatton, pictured in 1974 the year before her death

R.H.G. Tatton, his wife Maud and their daughter Susan

Above: This Statue of Oliver Cromwell once stood in Manchester, but is now housed facing Wythenshawe Hall which his troops conquered in the Civil War

The grounds of Wythenshawe Hall as they look today

Wythenshawe Hall pictured today

STOCKTON HEATH - A BYGONE ERA

by Herbert James Westbrook

£3

LOWTON - A BYGONE ERA

By Richard Ridyard

£3

FAREWELL HOWE BRIDGE

By Edna Aspden Lee

£3

CULCHETH - A BYONE ERA

Olive Watkin

£3

Any of these titles can be ordered direct from the publisher or through local bookshops